IF YOU ARE A CRACKER....
YOU PROBABLY BELIEVE
YOUR GRANDPARENTS COULD
WALK ON WATER

BY

Charlotte Crawford

Order this book online at www.trafford.com/
or email orders@trafford.com

Most Trafford titles are also available at major online book retailers.

Note for Librarians: A cataloguing record for this book is available from Library
and Archives Canada at www.collectionscanada.ca/amicus/index-e.html

Printed in Victoria, BC, Canada.

ISBN: 978-1-4120-5063-0 (sc)
ISBN: 978-1-4122-3286-9 (e)

*Our mission is to efficiently provide the world's finest, most comprehensive
book publishing service, enabling every author to experience success.
To find out how to publish your book, your way, and have it available
worldwide, visit us online at www.trafford.com/*

Trafford rev. 10/14/2009

www.trafford.com

North America & international
toll-free: 1 888 232 4444 (USA & Canada)
phone: 250 383 6864 ♦ fax: 812 355 4082

TABLE OF CONTENTS

Dedication   5

Foreword from Author   7

What Is a Cracker   9

If You Are Cracker   26

Grand Mama   44

Grand Daddy   49

Fried Cornbread   54

Eating Blackeyed Peas and Cornbread   57

Hog Proof Lunch Box   60

River of Peace   63

Anhingha   66

Orangrove   68

Panther   74

Grandma Dora   79

Baby in the Spring   91

I Am Worth Half a Hog   93

My Mother and Father Have an Office   97

Patchwork Quilt   105

Cracker Boy - Cracker Dog   108

Georgia Rain   112

A Further Attempt to Try to Explain
    a Few Things Maybe   114

Mama Brought the Last Crop In   123

References   129

About the Author   131

Dedicated

to

every

Cracker....

past

present

and

future....

with

blessings

from

Pembroke Hill

A foreword from the author....

Cracker is what I know best. I have enjoyed being a Cracker every minute of my life… and… I have enjoyed every Cracker I have known. I believe being a Cracker is a spiritual experience. We have insights to places other people do not seem to have. We were gifted with something special. I am not able to tell you exactly what that "something" is. I have come as close to it as I can by writing this book.

…Charlotte Crawford

What are Crackers?

Who are Crackers?

Where did they come from?

Where are they now?

What did they do?

What do they do now?

A Cracker is not a redneck. Cracker does not mean bigot. Somehow the meaning of Cracker got twisted and confused over a period of generations by a few people who did not know any better.

Cracker is the name of a Scots-Irish ethnic group that began migrating to the United States before 1900.

These are not the Irish people who landed in New York. They got yankeeized. Crackers arrived at Virginia, Georgia, North and South Carolina. Those who landed in Virginia migrated to North Carolina, to South Carolina, to Georgia and ultimately to Florida. Some went to Kentucky and Tennessee.

They got mountainized – or something like that. Florida Crackers who trace their ancestry learn each generation moved a little further South. It is hard to figure out what happened to the people who migrated to Alabama. But, in our hearts, we know they really are Crackers.

We seem to think of Crackers as living mostly in Florida and Georgia. It is difficult to determine how many Crackers came down to Florida as opposed to how many stayed in Georgia or the other "upper states". At one time Florida was made up mostly of Crackers. They got Baptized. The majority of Crackers settled in Georgia. They got canonized.

Almost everyone who migrated to Florida came down to get away from something or someone. Then, that something or someone they were trying to get away from would come down and take a whack at them.

People came to Florida to get away from slavery, other people, the government, the law, the military, people who believed in slavery and people who believed in abolition. Indians came down here to get away from white people, the government, soldiers and other Indians. Black people came down here to get away from slavery, white people, the government, soldiers, and, like Indians, they were trying to get away from oppression in general. It was Black people and Indians who first came to Florida as permanent residents. They got here before white people. It was white people they were trying to get away from.

Soldiers came to Florida to kill members of the other side, arrest men into the military, kill and whack Indians further South and pillage in general. Meanwhile, in the "upper states" the soldiers were busy beating Indians further and further West.

Bounty hunters came down here to capture runaway and freed slaves, AWOL soldiers, draft evaders, Indians, outlaws and anyone else who may have been worth a reward. Cow hunters came to Florida to make a fortune rounding up wild cows the Spanish left when they were the ones in Florida taking a whack out of everyone who happened to be here. The Indians were also interested in cows. The cow hunters whacked the Indians and the Indians whacked back the best they could. Even though the cows may have belonged to the Indians, the cow hunters made millions of dollars fattening up and selling them to all those people working up such an appetite whacking the daylights out of each other. If they sold cows to the Union they were not supposed to sell them to the Confederacy. If they sold cows to the Confederacy they were not supposed to sell them to the Union. No one was supposed to sell them to Cuba. The cow hunters who made the most money were the ones who sold to all three. One of those men was the man who at one time owned most of my home town. My high school was named after him.

The cow hunters were not the only ones who broke the rules. For example: the federal government would not let their soldiers come to Florida to wipe out a whole town of runaway slaves. So a general, who later became president of the United States, bribed a band of renegade Indians to come down here and massacre and burn down the town of Black people. Half of that tribe had already came down here to get away from the other half. Some of the Black people and Indians had been teaming up to protect each other. For some reason the soldiers did not like this. So the soldiers sent Indians down here to whack Black people while the soldiers whacked the Indians who had come down here to get away from it all. These are the same soldiers who later became the Union Army who fought the Confederate Army supposedly over slavery. Whack.

In the early 1800's the federal government gave white people land to come to Florida provided they would farm it and keep themselves armed and keep the Indians beaten to the Southern part of Florida – by shooting at them. Or: "Whack the Indians so we can get their land and cows."

By the middle of the eighteen hundreds Florida was made up of fugitives, felons, renegades, migrants, refugees and soldiers who were worse than the felons and renegades. Crackers were mostly migrants and refugees. They were looking for elbow room, peace and quiet, independence and, most of all, to get away from a government and soldiers that could be listed in the yellow pages under "thieves and murderers."

Crackers hated government intervention, rules or regulations of any kind. They especially hated its cruelty. That is one of the main reasons they left Europe in the first place. It is no wonder one of the first Territory of Florida flags had the motto: "Let Us Alone".

After the Civil War there was talk in Congress – and just talk – of giving Black people land that was owned by white people. One way or the other some Freedmen did wind up living on land once owned by white people. And, white men who had been a part of the Confederacy were not allowed to hold elected office while Black men could – and did. This caused misunderstanding and resentment that led to a tremendous amount of whacking that will probably never completely come to an end.

The icing on the cake was the carpet baggers who came from the North right after the Civil War. They came down here and took a whack out of peoples' ownership of their property. The carpet baggers bought out bankrupt property owners all over the South just for the amount of unpaid property taxes. A major whack. What the soldiers did not get, the carpet baggers got. Whack, whack, whack.

In the beginning the dinosaurs came down to Florida during the Ice Age to try to keep from freezing to death. The state became a dinosaur burial ground. This is much like the latter day Yankee retirees. Florida has now become a Yankee burial ground. The dinosaur bones made phosphate. So far, we have not found any use for the Yankee bones.

By the late eighteen-hundreds the federal government was running out of people to whack so in their infinite wisdom they sent the Army engineers to Florida to find a way to connect the St. John's River with the Peace River. They were running out of people so they decided to give the ground and the environment a great big whack and ruin it the best they could.

An Army engineer stumbled onto phosphate pebble in the Peace River. They dropped the idea of connecting the rivers – praise the Lord – and started whacking the daylights out of the dinosaur bones: phosphate. The beginning of the phosphate industry was the beginning of a major migration to Central Florida. "The Phosphate Rush". They have been whacking the Earth ever since.

The Crackers who came to Central Florida in the early 1900's to work in the phosphate mines came here mostly for the same reason: to keep from starving to death in Georgia, Alabama and North Florida. The citrus and cattle industries certainly brought their share of people to Florida but were a little more kind to the environment. Phosphate attracted more than its share of whacking.

Over the years Crackers remained a very hardy, ferociously independent, self reliant breed of people. They would have to have been to survive the carnage of the Civil War and hardships of "the wild and woolly South" that was Florida. Only the hardiest came to Florida and only the hardiest of the hardiest survived being here. Crackers who survived the evolution from the beginning to the present are as tough as whet leather.

Crackers are as strong and as reliable as the Clydesdale horses that are native to Scotland. They are made up of a great deal of down to earth common sense. Some seem to be born old and wise. They are also the most unpretentious and non-presumptuous people in the world. Most have a delightful sense of humor. It is almost impossible to tell rich Crackers from poor ones. They all look and act pretty much the same. There is no such thing as a Cracker putting on airs. They revere nature, embrace their heritage and worship their ancestors. No Cracker ever lived in vain.

Although Crackers strive to be self reliant, they are always there for friends and family when they are needed. They are also there when they are not needed. No one has to ask for help. Crackers look out for each other and will look out for anyone who will let them. This is in their genes. Their Scots-Irish ancestry makes them naturally clannish. The hardships of migration, the Civil War and all the whacking in general made Crackers develop a sense of looking out for each other. They had to in order to survive.

Although they are head strong and strong willed, and at times very feisty, they are also a very generous and caring people; but, they do not expect or ask for anything in return. They do not expect help from anyone even in times of their most desperate needs.

Crackers usually live their lives within bounds. Crackers trust themselves. In addition to looking out for each other they also keep each other straight. If Crackers see "jack legs" doing wrong they will try to straighten them out. If the "jack legs" do not straighten out the Crackers will just ignore them. It is an unwritten and unspoken rule that a Cracker has to be noble and maintain a certain level of dignity to remain worthy of the title Cracker.

It is a curious debate how Crackers got their name. The most common explanation is that the cow hunters in Florida, who had come down from Georgia, cracked their whips above the heads of the cows as they herded them from place to place. The crack of the whip could be heard for quite a distance. This explanation does not hold much water because most Crackers were not cow hunters. They were farmers and gatherers; and, people were called Crackers in Georgia before cow hunting became and industry in Florida.

A favorite explanation is that there was an abundance of peanuts in Georgia and Crackers got addicted to roasted or boiled peanuts and went around cracking and eating them much of the time. Crackers are a very food orientated people with tremendous appetites and it is amusing that eating may have something to do with why they were named Crackers.

Most likely and easiest to believe is that these jolly Scots–Irish people were all the time going around telling amusing stories and cracking jokes. Ironically, it may have been Black people who helped perpetuate the name "Cracker". Black lore tells us that Black people had, and still have, an art of sitting around and telling far-fetched and funny stories about each other. This is done good naturedly in their unique and graceful language. Black people have for many generation called this "crackin' someone". (Zora Neal Hurston, <u>Mules and Men</u>, New York: Harper

Perenial, 1990, p. 28). They also call this "telling tales" or "telling lies".

Websters Third New International Dictionary 1996, tells us:

> *"to crack: Scot. Talk, chat, gossip or to make a smart remark. A cracker is a thing or person of excellence. A cracker is a bragging liar, a boaster, one who quips or relates wittily."*

It appears the Scots–Irish brought the word Cracker with them when they migrated to this country. A recent interview with a native Britain tells us if someone is referred to as a cracker that means they are "a real go getter".

On September 4, 1999 on a British sit-com on PBS, "As Times Goes By", the character Rocky Hardcastle, age 84, said to his bride of 78 at the altar, commenting on her appearance, "You are a cracker!" He meant she is superior in everyway. On January 29, 2000 on the same sit-com a woman said of her live-wire boyfriend, "He is like a jumping cracker."

On April 15, 2000, two vivacious young women were called crackers because of their attractiveness.

The Compact Edition of the Oxford English Dictionary (Oxford University Press 1971) lists "crack" as a slang for pre-eminent, super excellent, first class and cites:

> *Young, Ann. Agric.*
> *(1793) XIX, 95. "[Sheep]*
> *a crack flock, which is a*
> *provincial term for excellent."*

The same dictionary lists "cracker" as one who or that which cracks and cites:

Dickens, Amer. Notes (1850) 14/1

> *"A teller of anecdotes and cracker of jokes."*

It also lists "cracker" as a boaster or braggart and cites:

> *Barclay, Shyp of Folys (1874) I 12 "Crakers*
> *and bosters with Courters auenterous."*

In Act II, Scene 1 of William Shakespeare's "The

Life and Death of King John" (first presented in 1596), the Duke of Austria said of Philip the Bastard (who was long-winded, bright, humorous, boastful and taunted people with his well placed words):

> *"What cracker is this same that deafs our ears with his abundance of superfluous breath?"*

This is the most scholastic explanation for the presence of the word here in America. The word certainly was not created here and then taken back to Great Britain. This explanation should sit with more credence with historians rather than all those dozens of over-simplified theories.

The same dictionary goes on to tell us that poor white Southerners may have been called Crackers. If so, this would have included a tremendous number of people. Some were born rich. Some were born poor, worked very hard then became rich. Would a person stop being a Cracker when they became rich? What if a rich person lost his fortune? Would he then become a Cracker? Rich or poor makes no sense.

Let it be known: all Scots-Irish people who migrated to the Southern states are Crackers, rich and poor alike and the only acceptable and accurate definition of Cracker is: people of excellence who tell great stories and have a lot to boast about – especially their food.

The saddest commentary about the word is all the negative connotations it has been given over the generations here in the United States. The latest blow was the death knell dealt to it during the civil rights struggles in the 1960's. People and the press needed a nick-name for the Southern racial bigots. The word "Cracker" was the handiest, even won out over "red-neck". These people should check their history, dictionaries and talk to people from Great Britain. They will find out they are sorely mistaken. They took a whack out of our identity.

This author has also grown weary of the Frederick Remington's drawings of Crackers or cow hunters with the droopy-head-hanging-down horse, the droopy-head-hanging-down—cow poke, with the huge brim drooping down hat. I contend these are characteratures exaggerated for commercial appeal. This is in as bad taste as the characteratures of Black people and Native Americans we are all familiar with. Cowboys in Florida did not look that much different from cowboys in Wyoming. Keep in mind that Remington loved the West and hated the South, especially Central Florida. He found the people, farmers and cowboys absolutely repulsive. He was here only for a few weeks but we have had to live with his snap vision for one-hundred years. (Cinnamon Bair. The Ledger, March 21, 2000, section D, page 1) The best thing we can do is just completely ignore Frederick Remington. He took a whack out of our image.

In the final analysis, it does not matter how Crackers got their name, but it is very important we have a name. It does not matter whose definition of a Cracker someone believes because if someone is a Cracker they will know it and other Crackers will recognize them right away. No one can ever take a whack out of these instincts. On the other hand, if someone is not a Cracker they will never know what they are missing. They will never know.

IF YOU ARE A CRACKER
YOU PROBABLY....

believe your grandparents could walk on
water.

never go to someone's house without
bringing them a gift – usually food or
flowers.

do not want a lot of frills or material things.

live about the same while you are rich as you
did when you were poor.

enjoy repairing something that is old more
than buying something new.

would rather eat at home than at a fancy

restaurant.

do not like "R" rated movies.

drive slowly so you can look at the trees,
flowers, cows or lakes or what ever might be
out there.

are sentimental about houses your families
have lived in.

know how to cook almost everything from
scratch.

had rather sit by the lake than to go to
Disney World.

would crawl on your hands and knees for
a mile in a hurricane to repay someone so
much as a nickel you owe them.

are very kind to people you respect and are
even civil to people you do not respect.

have a temper if you get really riled.

do not get really riled very often.

feel like crying when a spring dries up.

feel like crying when a big tree is cut down.

cry when an animal dies.

always take very good care of your children.

are very generous – even to strangers.

never engage in pretense.

do not go around wanting something you
can not have.

know a lot about the Christian religion.

love music.

love to dance.

love to sing.

and most of all – love to tell stories.

keep really good recipes a family secret.

never stand on formality – but always use good manners.

do not acknowledge different classes of people.

can walk up to total strangers and start talking to them as if you have known them all your life.

love a good debate.

give people the benefit of the doubt until they prove themselves otherwise.

know your wife is every bit as smart as you are and ask her advice on almost everything.

know that you are smarter than your husband but wait for him to ask your advice on almost everything.

usually let the other guy get the better end of

a deal.

eat fresh vegetables everyday.

are kin to someone who lives in the state of Georgia.

visit grave sites at the cemetery.

know a lot about your family tree.

never take unfair advantage of anyone – not even your enemies.

dearly love to hear yourself say, "thank you".

dearly love to hear yourself say, "you are welcome".

have given away as much as you have kept.

believe the most important thing in your life is your heritage.

try to teach young people what they need to

know.

appreciate your elders for teaching you what you need to know.

have never been fired for shoddy work.

know a person does not have to do a lot or travel far to have a good life.

believe in individuality. Do not particularly believe in majority rule.

know when to keep your mouth shut.

are real good at laughing.

are real good at crying.

are capable of making yourself do chores you do not want to do.

chalk things up you do not understand as "the nature of the beast."

are determined to be temperate and in control of yourself.

are pretty good at adjusting when you have to.

feel better sitting under a tree than in a house.

know that simplicity will comfort your soul.

are very tenacious but know that if something gets to be too much trouble then maybe it is best to just not do it.

figure there are two kinds of people: those with dignity and those without dignity.

know that individual responsibility is what ensures the continuity of civilization.

thoroughly enjoy work – good old satisfying work.

always have iced tea with lunch and dinner.

think something really great has happened
when a flower blooms.

know how to peel and cut up sugar cane to
chew and have chewed it.

do not charge interest when you loan money
to a friend.

always show elderly people a lot of respect.

know someone who is a member of Eastern
Star.

have never eaten greens without corn bread
and never will.

love to browse around in old, very old
hardware stores.

stop dead in your tracks when you see a
rainbow.

stand up for your rights.

stand up for other peoples' rights.

have too much pride to lie.

had rather swap or trade than to buy or sell.

know someone who is very rich.

know someone who is very poor.

can remember almost everything you did
when you were a child.

like movies that have horses in them.

would dearly love the woods and forest to
remain pristine.

remember how your grandmother smelled.

would rather do almost anything yourself
than to pay someone to do it.

will pay someone to do something you
could do yourself just to help them out of a

financial bind.

would never tell anyone how much money you have.

believe clothes should be made only of cotton or wool.

have a Bible that is older than you are.

know that fried white bacon and rice with tomato gravy are always served together.

always over pay someone a little bit when they do some work for you.

have parents who tell you stories about their parents and grandparents.

have children who ask you to tell them stories about their grandparents and great grandparents.

never say someone is ugly.

know that when you are dealing with people you have to be willing to give them a lot of slack.

treat people who work for you like members of the family.

are convinced the Civil War should not have happened.

know the names of just about every fruit, vegetable, flower and tree there is.

have slept under a hand sewn patchwork quilt.

never walk past a garden without taking a good long look.

remember your first grade teacher very vividly. SHE TAUGHT YOU HOW TO READ!

plant as much as possible every spring even

though you no longer live on a farm.

never take the last serving of anything. You always leave it for someone else.

have tools and utensils that have been in your family for generations.

know what "root hog or die" means.

know at least five different ways to "fix" an orange for eating.

much prefer to live in a house that is older than you.

enjoy any kind of gathering as long as it includes food.

know the difference between a palmetto bush and a palm tree.

think it is funny when you know someone is trying to pull something over on you because you know they can not do it.

are related to a lot of people who have worked in the phosphate mines in the state of Florida.

love the sound of a Southern accent.

know better than to argue with a member of your family. It is very habit forming and always just gets worse and worse.

wish the future would be just like the past.

believe it is an honor for people to call you by your first name with a "Mister" or a "Miss" in front of it.

are certain vegetables grown in the yard taste a lot better than the ones bought in the store.

are fully aware of the tragedy of human beings encroaching on the habitat of wild animals.

believe in being on time. Lateness is rudeness.

are always looking forward to something you have planted to sprout.

always listen when people talk.

know where it will take place when someone says, "all day sing with dinner on the grounds".

would like to be able to do everything yourself. Build your own house, drill your own well, grow your own food, produce your own power, cut your own hair. Build or create everything you need or want and maintain it all by yourself.

are convinced the best way to cook fish is to roll it in meal and then fry it in shallow oil until it is crispy.

have a very special fondness for things made

of real wood.

love to hear the sounds of animals.

love to hear the sounds of weather.

do not believe in modern day urgencies –
fast food – fast communications – fast mail
– "what is the hurry?".

found that rising above racial prejudice was
one of the easiest thing you have ever done.

always say, "Hey. How are you doing?" to
everyone you see.

pull for both sides when two people are in a
squabble. You really hope they both get what
they need or want.

bake cookies for the church bazaar and then
go to the bazaar and buy your own cookies.

wash, dry and put away the dishes
immediately after each meal.

are not afraid of bugs.

do not understand how anyone could eat
good food and not believe in God.

are capable of tending to business and chores
as usual when something tragic is going on
in your life.

always clean and mop when you move out of
a house.

always clean and mop when you move into a
house.

always make certain when you borrow
something it is in better shape when you
return in than when you borrowed it.

learned how to do some of your cooking
from a Black woman.

can not believe the company would put
Coca-Cola in anything other than the small

green bottles.

know the contentment of sitting on a porch
– rocking in a rocker or swinging in a swing.

have done a tremendous amount of work if
you are a man.

have done even more work if you are a
woman.

believe anyone who does a good job raising
children will get a seat on the first row in
heaven.

do not drive on the inter-state highways. You
always take the back roads – the roads that
are blue on the map. "Take the blue roads".

feel the dearest people in the world to you
are other Crackers.

wish frozen french fries had never been
invented.

sit out in the yard and talk to your neighbors
often.

know someone who has picked cotton.

spend a great deal of time explaining things
to people who are not Crackers.

know what a "he coon" is.

know who Lawton Chiles is.

believe small towns should stay small.

believe most Crackers are honorable.

believe most Crackers are humble.

believe most Crackers are noble.

believe your grandparents could walk on
water.

GRAND MAMA

She knew something we did not know.

I could not tell where the talcum powder left off and the flour began. Hugging her was like hugging a warm feather mattress that smelled like a spring bouquet and a loaf of fresh baked bread.

Everything about her was soft. Her skin was soft. Her dress and apron were soft from having been washed, run through a ringer and dried in the sunny breeze countless times. I did not think anything could be more soft and tender to touch – but it did. Her night gown and bed linens were even more soft than her dress and apron. They were cotton puff soft. She walked softly. She spoke softly. And, nothing ever changed.

Grand Mama was born in 1892, appropriately

on Christmas morning. She was a special gift to us and she had special gifts of her own.

The only song I ever heard from her was "Silent Night" - in the form of a soft, quiet whisper of a whistle as she worked in her kitchen. And, that was only the first two bars. Silent night…Holy night. She went about her chores like something floating through this life on a cloud.

There was no doubt she knew at a very early age exactly how she was going to spend the rest of her life and she was determined to go about it with grace and dignity. She never complained. She never raised her voice. She never showed anger. When one of her sons would not mind she would deliberately say, "Gentle Men!"

She chose to live plain. She did not want a lot of stuff. She kept house with the same furniture she and Grand Daddy set up house keeping with around 1909. She said time and time again, "I do not want anything I do not have to have." And she meant it. She never had many clothes at a time – a few plain dresses, maybe a dress-up dress or two, one pair of everyday shoes, one pair of dress-up shoes, one pair of bedroom slippers, one coat.

How could someone who never had but the barest necessities have the wisdom to avoid the burden and frustration of materialism? Her formal education had ended at age fifteen. She was born wise. She somehow knew simplicity would caress her soul with peace and comfort.

She had one luxury she enjoyed as much as anyone could ever enjoy anything: her love for animals. She loved cats. She loved dogs. She loved all animals. She said many times, "I even like an old hog." She made no demands. The animals made no demands. They made spiritual contact. They were soul mates. Her children and grand children were absolutely everything to her. She adored her husband. They all thought she was some kind of goddess. Everything was referred to "Grand Mama" – "What would Grand Mama think."

Her super natural wisdom was matched only by her super natural ability to prepare food – as she did while quietly whisper whistling the first two bars of

"Silent Night". Everything she cooked and served was always perfect. The food never varied. Each dish always looked and tasted exactly the same as the last time she served it. There were no mistakes. There were no goof ups.

I was in awe of her temperance, deliberateness and her being in complete control. I am still overwhelmed by the vision of this perfect human being sitting at her kitchen table grating fresh coconut to sprinkle over top of her made from scratch butter cake with her made from scratch white icing while quietly whisper whistling "Silent night…Holy night" – but only the first two bars. She did not even need the whole song. Just the first two bars.

It seems like she knew something we do not know – and she never really told us what it was. She was not one to talk a lot and it was obvious she knew more than she told. (She would sometimes say, "Don't tell everything you know. If you do then everyone will know everything you know.") Was it that simplicity is godliness and animals are closer to God than human beings are and they are our conduit to the Best

Place? Perhaps that was her bounty, her gold she held in reserve in a world that was her very own. Her favorite scriptures were "…your Father prepares many mansions for you in heaven"…and, where God said to the materialistic man, "Thou fool!" Maybe that is why she did not want her home and her life cluttered with stuff and more stuff. She wanted to keep a clear, uncluttered vision to her mansion and treasures that were somewhere else.

We believe she is in her mansion in heaven with her animals and she is quietly going about her chores while softly whistling, "Silent night…Holy night." But, just the first two bars.

She knew something we do not know.

GRAND DADDY

He was as hardy as the Clydesdale horses native to his grand father's Scotland. He was a large man. He had to be. No small body could have held the amount of jolliness, generosity, love and affection he showered on everyone and everything that was fortunate enough to be in his path. He made people laugh. He told stories. He cracked jokes. He made people happy with his glorious smile that beamed between his two chubby fat cheeks.

He never met a stranger. Everyone who worked for him was glad he was one of the bosses at the phosphate mines. He never had any serious problems with any of his workers. They wanted to work for him. He took care of them. As it was at the time when someone went to work for "the mines" they became a members of the mines family. They were taken care of – looked after. No one ever went without basic needs. No one was wealthy but no one was desperately poor. Most people who worked at the mines lived in phosphate villages built near the mines by the companies that owned them. This gave the employees a strong sense of community and belonging. Everyone felt at home because they were at home and they knew it.

One of Grand Daddy's jobs was to travel to one of the offices some 50 miles south of the village of Pembroke. Every week he would stop at a flower farm and bring back a car load – literally stacked from floor to ceiling – of flowers. Sometimes he brought back gladiolas, sometimes roses. He would stop at peoples' houses and leave large beautiful bouquets. Everyone was working folks but from time to time they had the same flowers in their homes as the wealthiest people. Thanks to Grand Daddy.

His generosity was exceeded only by his festive notions about food. He loved food. His world revolved around food – and people. More food and more people. On regular occasions he invited some

100-200 people to his home up on the hill for picnics. This was a company house that included several acres shaded by giant oak trees. Sometimes it was for birthday parties, Christmas parties or just because the sun had risen and set. Sunday afternoons in the Summers might find a couple of hundred people up there just for "a watermelon cuttin'". They visited and ate watermelon in the shade of the great oak trees.

He had the men at the company shop build a fifty foot long picnic table complete with electric lights and a set of swings for the children – of all ages. There was a bar-be-que pit and a large smoker sometimes filled with fresh mullet from the Gulf. The picnic table, the dinning table and the ping pong table on the porch were filled with food. Most of the food was covered dishes brought by his friends. And the air was filled with the aroma of FOOD. And, it was good.

He did not have to do any of this. He did it because he loved food and he loved people – and he loved them even more when they were all together.

In his mother's own words, "He is noble". There is no doubt his inspiration and motivation came at least partly from the fact that he was married to my grandmother. Although she was as quiet and passive as he was boisterous and aggressive it was obvious he was very excited over the fact that he was married to "Miss Ethel".

Grand Mama was his shining light and she was certain he was the husband of all husbands. His children saw him as the deity of all deities and were in absolute awe of him, especially my father, his oldest child. For his whole life my father referred, deferred, measured and compared everything to Grand Daddy. Everything.

Grand Daddy could be stern at times. He would put his foot down and would be boss when a boss was needed. His workers nor children never minded. He was boss and he was adored.

If any of his workers had ever looked up and had seen Grand Daddy walking across the top of the water of the settling pond no one would have been the least bit surprised. No one would have even so much as flinched. Some people believed Grand Daddy was the second coming.

Sometimes I wonder if perhaps they were right.

FRIED CORN BREAD

This is not a cook book.
This is Cracker lore.

Some people know the secrets to making the best fried corn bread in the whole world and some people do not. A perfect fried corn bread patty is a little piece of heaven but it has to be done right.

The secrets are:

The water must be BOILING when poured into the mix to make sure the flour and the meal melt together.

The edges of the patty must be fried twice.

Self rising flour must be used.

White cream meal must be used.

The bread tastes better if your mother's or your grandmother's finger prints are on the patties.

To begin:

Mix about half and half meal and flour very thoroughly.

Use a large bowl.

Add a pinch of salt.

Some people like to add onion to the mix. Onion is not necessary in the bread because the onion actually tastes better if eaten on the side. If you put onion in the bread just use a small amount and make sure it is chopped very fine. Onion has a tendency of making the bread a little bit watery after it is cooked.

Make a crater in the bowl of mixture and pour the <u>boiling</u> water into the middle of crater a little at a time and mix into the center of bowl until the mixture is a thick, stiff paste. Let cool until able to handle.

Form patties a little less smaller than the palm of your hand and about 7/16 of an inch thick. Rinse hands in cold water and/or flour hands to keep patties from sticking to palms. Be sure and leave a three finger impression on each patty.

The oil in the frying pan should be a hair less deep than the thickness of the patty.

The oil should be very hot before adding the first patty. The patty should begin to fry as soon as you put it in the oil. Two or three patties can be fried at the same time as long as the oil stays good and hot.

The purpose of the oil being just to the top of the patty but not over the top is to make sure the top and bottom are fried once while the edges are fried twice.

Fry until the edges and bottoms are brown and the patty is firm enough to turn with spatula. Do not use tongs.

Turn only once. Tops and bottoms will be golden brown and edges a darker brown and crispy. Drain on paper towels.

In present days people vary on preference of cooking oil. Peanut oil, safflower oil. I prefer Crisco.

Of course the best tasting oil is bacon grease.

Eating Black-eyed Peas
and Fried Cornbread

There is not a right way or a wrong way to eat black-eyed peas and fried corn bread, although some ways are better than others. Since eating black-eyed peas and fried corn bread is such a spiritual experience there really should be some documentation on it. So I will tell you what I believe is the best way.

First of all it is easy to cook black-eyed peas. I recommend using fresh peas with plenty of snaps. Whether you use fresh or dried peas just put them in a pot of water and let them simmer until they are tender. (forty five minutes to an hour) You can season them how you wish but peas are not peas unless they are cooked with some kind of pork. It is smart to use bacon that had been cooked or lean ham. Bacon fat tastes best even if it is more deadly. Peas need little or no salt. Put in a bay leaf to bring out the natural sodium taste of the peas.

To eat: put the peas in a bowl the size of an average soup bowl. The pot licker depth should be at least a quarter of an inch above the peas and there should be a few slivers of pork floating around in the pot licker. Eat with a table spoon.

Some people cut up yellow onions, green peppers and tomatoes into small pieces and put them into the bowl with the peas. I do not believe in doing this. A bowl of peas is sacred. Putting anything in the bowl with them would be a distraction. I find it much better to eat the peas by themselves and keep a small onion with the green handle on it laying beside the bowl and take a bite of it when I feel it is time for a bite of raw onion. It tastes a bit more heavenly this way.

To begin:

First, sip a couple of spoons full of pot licker to get your mouth started.

(2) bite off the edge of a fried cornbread patty, chew and wash down with another spoonful or two of pot licker.

(3) take a spoonful of peas, chew and swallow.

(4) dunk cornbread down into peas and pot licker, bite and chew with a spoonful of peas.

(5) put the cornbread down and take a bite of onion.

(6) repeat the above in the order or reverse order or any varied order until the peas and pot licker are a shallow puddle in the bottom of the bowl.

(7) using the back of your spoon, press the remaining peas into a paste, crumble some of the cornbread into it and eat the mixture with the spoon.

(8) take a piece of cornbread with the edge bitten off and wipe clean the remaining divine dampness in the bottom of the bowl and eat the cornbread.

You will need some iced tea to go with all this.

The Hog Proof Lunch Box

"The hogs ate my lunch!" That is what my father told his parents in 1918. He was in second grade at a two-room schoolhouse in Homeland. He lived in the phosphate village of Pembroke where there was no school and had the option of attending a few miles north at Homeland or a few miles south at Ft. Meade. The only horse and buck board buggy that left Pembroke went to Homeland and he was on it.

Homeland was not a phosphate village but a community that had its origins in the Methodist Church camp meetings that grew into a tiny town with a church, post office, school and general store. The church established the school that later became a part of the public school system. Lucky for my father there was a horse and buggy to the Homeland school because the two years he attended there was among his favorite. He never stopped talking about it.

My father carried his lunch to school in a square, stiffer than card board, lunch box that had a lid tied down with a flat cotton cord. He would lay it on the ground to go play before school took in. The lunch box worked just fine under ordinary circumstances but it was easy prey for the neighborhood hogs that would get loose and run around the schoolyard. They would root the lunch box open and eat his sandwich and cookies.

To a Crawford, absolutely, the most important thing in the whole world is food. My grandfather could not stand for his son to go all day at school with no lunch. This was serious business. He knew what he had to do and swung into action.

He cut a flat pattern out of copper mesh, folded and shaped it like the soft lunch box, fastened the sides together with rivet like brads, made the same shaped lid that was held in place with a leather strap and metal buckle. The soft lunch box was carried inside the metal one.

61

From then on my father carried his lunch to school in this contraption. It worked perfectly. He said the hogs would still try to get in it but all they could do was roll it around the schoolyard with their snouts.

When my brother was elected to the Florida Legislature in 1978 our mother had the lunch box silver plated and a new strap put on it for him to take to Tallahassee. We had heard there was a lot of pork barreling going on up there and we were afraid this meant there would be some old hogs running around in the yard at the Capitol Building and would get his lunch. The hog proof lunch box still works just fine.

River of Peace

Cypress soldiers standing guard
with
long Jehovah beards hanging down
created
in His own image

Secrets hidden in the black
muddy water
moving slowly
moving slowly

Precious stones removed
long ago
What more do you hold?
is it for us to know
or

just to wonder

We stand and watch you flow
quietly
we walk along your banks
of
rich black mud
never furrowed
never planted

Why are you here?
you have given us
so much
why are we here?
we haven't done
a thing for you
except
take a whack out of
your innards

For a hundred years
we have let you

rest in peace
and you give us Peace,
River

Anhingha

Anhingha
let me sing a
song for you.
Let me stay by
let me fly by
your side.
Take me higher
ever neigher
to God.
Searching for living water
soaring higher
ever higher
widening circles
Anhingha
Where do you go

Anhingha?
Following no trail
leaving no tracks.
Where do you go?
touching wings with
the Great Holy Mystery?
I am one
Return anhingha
return.
We together
a part of everything
a part of everywhere.
Everything holy.
Everything sacred.
Land, sky, sea
you and me
Anhingha

Orangrove

The Mystery Cat

Turning off the paved road it was less than a quarter mile up the steep hill to my Grand Parents' house, set in a heavenly oak hammock. A short distance further was a large orange grove owned by the same company that owned the hill and the two large houses set apart by perhaps seventy-five yards. It was the kind of cozy setting people dream about. The houses could not be seen from the road but most everyone for miles around knew who lived up there because they had been there at one time or another for cook outs and picnics. From time to time people would pay extra visits the occupants of the houses did not know about and drop off unwanted cats and kittens. Of course the orphans found their way to my

Grand Mama's house by the aroma of her cooking. She loved cats and all animals. She fed and talked to them. They sat on her lap as she sat on one of the big comfortable wicker rocking chairs on the front porch. Favorites sometimes came into the house. Most of the cats were all pretty much the same. They were cats. They looked like cats. They acted like cats. Of course Grand Mama gave them names. There was a solid black one that was sort of grumpy she named "Old Thing" and a beautiful white male she named "Tom". Tom was the last cat she had and was her favorite. They were very close. She had him for years and unlike the other cats she had in the past, he was taken to the veterinarian for shots and neutering. Tom was the only cat she had for the last number of years she lived and he enjoyed an "only cat's life" with her.

There had been many cats before Tom over a period of some fifty years – several at a time. All the cats stayed around the house most the time. They may have gone into the grove for a while or wandered around the acres of land that surrounded the two houses but they spent most of their time near the house and for the most part were all pretty much the same – as far as cats go – except for one. He came to the house as a young cat like the others but that was where the similarity ended. He looked like no cat had ever looked. He acted like no cat had ever acted. He did not have anything to do with the other cats. Most the cats played together, ate together and slept together – and Lord knows – would often breed and have kittens together. But not the cat my Grand Mama named Orangrove. When he first showed up it was assumed he had been dumped and had come up the hill as usual. But on re-thinking Orangrove, the mystery cat, we have decided perhaps he came from some place no one has been before. He did not look like anything we had seen. His tail and the top of his head looked like a tabby cat but the rest of his coat looked more like sheeps' wool. His eyes did not look like cats' eyes. They looked like human eyes. His mouth did not look like a cat's mouth. It looked like a human mouth. He was huge. Twice the size of the other cats. He did not eat with the cats. When he was eating the cats stayed away from the platter. He never showed any interest in mating with the cats and never showed signs of being pregnant or having had kittens. We do not even know if Orangrove was male or female. He never went into the house and he did not sit on Grand Mama's lap. She never even petted him.

Orangrove would come to the house and eat most days. Once in a while he would miss a day. He would hang around for a while and then walk slowly back into the grove even though there were plenty of places for cats to live and sleep around the house. There was the porches, under the house, a garage, a pump house and oak trees with big wide limbs that cats like. Orangrove probably went through the grove and into the woods beyond. A citrus grove bed is just sand and orange tree branches are not big enough to sleep on. He spent most of his time a long way from the house – perhaps even beyond the beyond. He seemed to know exactly what he wanted and where he wanted to go. After his short visits he would walk slowly back in the grove and disappear

– then re-appear in a day or so. This went on for the better part of a decade until the time he no longer came to the house.

What was he? Where did he go? And most of all, where did he come from? It would be appropriate to believe he was some kind of divine placement because The Hill was really cat heaven and was such a beautiful and spiritual place for all living things human and animal. If Orangrove was some of deity he was obviously in the right place. This leads to the question: "Why was he there on The Hill?". Maybe to show us that something like him does exist and The Hill was one of very few places where he could manifest? Something that looked like Orangrove would not appear just anywhere and if The Hill was a sacred place I am certain it was because of the presence of my Grand Parents.

A cat fancier took one look at Orangrove's picture and said, "Looks like the cat from hell". Some people believe a demonic spirit can appear as anything it wants to. IF this is true and he was trying to appear as a cat then ol' Orangrove sort of missed the mark. Close but not quite.

Orangrove showed us we do not have the answers to some things – and this is good. He also showed us The Hill was such a tremendously special place that something this different could be drawn to it, accepted, named, fed, remembered and written about sixty years later.

Panther

At Grand Mama's house
we heard a panther scream-
down by the stream.
We were up on the hill
but we had to go
down to the stream
to find that Panther we heard scream.

Run, Bobby, run.
Never mind the gun.
Watch every shadow.
Check every limb.
Don't let the panther find us
before we find him.

Bobby ran North.

I ran South with all my might.
A fool thing to do.
Separating in the woods
can mean a very lonely night.

I wanted to see the panther
more than I wanted to breathe.
I thought if I missed him
I wouldn't do nothin' but grieve.
I wanted to be the first
to lay eyes on that screaming panther.

And before I could think maybe I wouldn't –
there he was.
Up wind.

Watching a rabbit.
Not seeing me.

Right then I knew I did not
want him to see me.
Not because I was afraid –

but because I knew he had
never seen the likes of me
and if he did it would make
him less than perfect.
I whispered softly,
"Please don't look at me.
Seeing me would just diminish you."
I saw the panther
and I saw God.
I could not stop looking at him.

Please let me look away –
and not take away from this
Holy Beast.
I turned and ran North.
I ran with my eyes closed.
I did not want to look at anything
ever again ---
not after seeing that majestic thing.

I told Bobby I did not see the panther
down my way.

Better luck next time.
Grand Mama is calling us.
We better go.
It is supper time.

Laying in bed that night…
With my eyes closed…
I could still see the panther.
I would always see the panther…
I wish I had not seen him.
I am just glad he did not see me.

At Grand Mama's house…
way up on a hill…
surrounded by groves…
beyond the groves…
pristine woods.
A night with no moon…
pitch dark…
black…
nothing moving…
no sound…

still.

Far, far away…

just barely…

we heard a panther scream…

Grandma Dora

I never met her. She died when I was two months old. But, as it turns out, I know her as well, if not better, than I know anyone. She died in 1937 and my mother has never stopped talking about her. There has never been more than a week or two gone by that my mother has not told me something about her "Mama". Anytime we cook, plant or make something she tells me how "Mama" did it. I'm glad she does. It is obvious her Mama was the most endeared and most important person in my mother's life.

My mother was only twenty-two years old and had just had her first child when her Mama died. And, there was a time when her Mama was the only thing my mother and her siblings had.

Dora's life started out difficult, got a little better, then got a whole lot worse. The difficulties started long before she was born. Her ancestors were Irish famine immigrants. Her grandmother was raped by a Yankee soldier. This event produced her mother. Dora was born in 1883 in Sale City, Georgia. Her mother died in child birth two years later. Yes, Dora's mother was conceived in a rape and then died in child birth at age twenty-two. A beginning and ending that would give anyone pause upon learning about it.

Dora's father promptly re-married and had two more children. When she was seven years old her father was killed by gun shot. He and his neighbor shot each other to death over an argument about some horses. Dora was raised by aunts. Life was not easy in rural South Georgia in the 1890's. Dora's life was difficult enough that she did not talk about it much to her children but throughout her life she always persevered.

Dora must have applied herself and got a pretty good education because she helped her children with their school work – sitting by the light of the fire in the fire place. Dora had talents. She could play any musical instrument and could make things like children's toys.

"Mama was a lot of fun when she wasn't tired."

She could prepare any kind of food including canning and making butter. She could sew any kind of clothes. She seemed to know just about everything a person could know at that time and place. I've often wondered how she could get so smart. It was just her. She was special. Morally she was as superior as her talents and was always very good to her children.

"They don't come any better than Mama."

Dora was married around age twenty. Her in-laws were very fine people. The jury is still out on Dora's husband. Her father-in-law gave each of his four boys large parts of his very large farm in Camilla. Dora and her husband, Jesse, started out with about fifty acres, a new house, a barn, horses and several houses where Black workers lived. The oldest had been slaves, the younger might as well had been. They weren't going anywhere. All this was paid for free and clear. Great grandpa had a saw mill so constructing buildings was not too difficult.

Dora married Jesse in 1903. Twenty-three years and nine children later that farm was gone. Jesse was a spree drinker. He would go off for days at a time. Money got spent, bills did not get paid, money got borrowed and not paid back. His father surely got tired of bailing him out. It is not clear what happened to the farm. I don't know if the bank got it or if members of his family took it over but the farm was gone. It was 1926 and on top of everything else the bottom had fallen out of farm prices.

Starting out in 1903 the farm did fairly well. And it should have. There was plenty of farm hands to do the heaviest work and there were no debts. But, the more time went by and the more children Dora had to feed the worse it got.

Dora's first child was born a little more than a year after she was married. When the little girl was almost three years old she died of injuries from burns. Her floor length dress caught fire at the fire place and she took off running.

"Mama couldn't catch her in time."

Dora gave birth to children from 1904 until 1925. The youngest was only one year old when they left the farm and came down to Leesburg, Florida. Her oldest three children had families of their own by now but there was still five children at home.

They moved to Leesburg because their oldest son had already come down to work in a grocery store owned by one of the aunts and uncles that had raised Dora.

Dora and Jesse rented a large two story house and took in boarders. Jesse was lucky to get a job laying bricks for a new Baptist church. Damaged fruit and vegetables from the grocery store came in mighty handy. But, by 1928 the depression had set in real bad. There was no work. Even the boarders could not pay.

Things must have been mighty bad in Florida to make going back to South Georgia to a small rented farm look good. Dora and Jesse and their five youngest children moved to a farm in Moultrie where they were share croppers, pure and simple.

The first year was at least okay because they did

well enough to move to a farm they rented at a flat rate. The owner of all of these farms was also the owner of the grocery and general store. This came in handy to charge everything until the crops came in.

The new place had a big house and a beautiful view. There was a barn near the house with an apartment. This was a tobacco farm and the tobacco curing barn was down by the fields.

Things may have looked up at least a little but by December of 1929 Dora's husband was desperately ill. Alcohol had long since taken his health. He had a horrible gum infection that led to pneumonia. He also had kidney disease. Jesse died on a cold day in January 1930 at the age of 50.

My mother was the next to oldest at home. She was fourteen, her older brother sixteen, younger brother twelve, sisters were seven and five. My mother's oldest brother left the farm within the next few months. He went back down to Leesburg to live with his older brother and work at the grocery store. It seems if he had stayed he could have been good help. But he did not. This made my mother the oldest at home.

The work and accomplishments that took place over the next several months could have only happened at that time, at that location, under those circumstances and only with the efforts of my Grandma Dora and my mother – with some help from the younger brother and sisters. It happened because Dora and my mother were there together.

The fields were plowed and the tobacco plants planted because neighbor farmers usually helped each other. In addition to five acres of tobacco there was about forty-five acres of cotton, corn and peanuts. There was also the cooking of meals, laundry done by hand and the tending to the vegetable garden.

Dora hired a married couple to help but it was she who over saw the whole operation. She knew when to plant and what to plant, when to fertilize, when to top and when to harvest and how to cure. One of the jobs the children had was to go into the fields with a stick and knock the worms off the tobacco and the weevils off the cotton and stomp them to death on the ground. They did not have pesticides. They had to use the stick and stomp method. By this time my mother only had one dress that would fit to wear to school.

"Mama washed and starched and ironed it every night so I could wear it to school the next day."

The farm was about the same as the other farms they had lived on. There was no electricity or plumbing. They were lucky to have a well or a pump near by.

Tobacco was harvested around June of the year so at least my mother and her brother got to finish the school year. Back then they harvested the leaves only as they matured, taking the lower, larger leaves first and so on. There were at least three harvests that year.

Knowing my mother and knowing Grandma Dora I can assure there was a tremendous amount of work they did to bring that crop in. It was still up to Dora to get all this done – even with the help of the brother, sisters and the hired couple. I know my mother would have followed her Mama to the ends of the earth and did everything she could do to help, trying to do as much work as Mama.

Dora taught my mother how to work and she continued to work just like her Mama. The work she did in her and my father's law office, the work she does around our home, the million miles of afghans she has crocheted to sell at service club's bazaars has kept her Mama's spirit alive.

"Mama brought that last crop in all by herself."

I know it is true that crop would not have gotten in if Dora had not been there to make it happen but I am sure she had a lot of help from my mother. Dora used to say:

"Lucy is my angel from heaven."

After the tobacco leaves were cut and gathered they were tied together with string using a slip knot on each stem. The bunches of leaves were draped over wooden rods that hung in the barn. Dora cured each harvest of tobacco with graduated heat that took about two weeks. The barn was heated by a wood fire built in a furnace that was like a large pipe that went through the wall of the barn to the inside.

Although the fire could be stoked from the outside she still had to go inside the barn to see the progress of the curing. There was a thermometer not too far inside the barn door.

This process started out at about ninety degrees and was gradually raised to about one-hundred-thirty degrees. The appearance and texture of the leaves told when to raise the temperature. If the temperature got too low she had to stoke the fire. If it got too hot she had to pull some of the fire out of the furnace. This had to be watched closely twenty-four hours a day for about two weeks for each picking.

The cotton, corn and peanuts were harvested before and after the tobacco. Dora sent a wagon to town to bring back a lot of Black people to pick cotton and the other harvests. They were paid about a penny a pound for picking cotton and were paid daily. Dora had to meet a payroll. The whole family helped with all the picking including the cotton, the most difficult.

Dora sold the tobacco and the other crops for enough money to pay the bills for the year and to get her and her four remaining children back to Florida. They lived sometimes in Leesburg with Dora's oldest son and in Ft. Meade with her oldest daughter who was married to a man employed by the phosphate mines. Dora sewed for everyone. She made a lot of clothes and what ever they needed. She lived for seven years after coming back to Florida. Died at the early age of fifty-four.

"Mama worked herself to death."

After living their last year in Georgia farming in poverty, there is something poetic in that after just one short generation my mother's son, Dora's grandson, became Commissioner of Agriculture of the State of Florida, a member of the governor's cabinet. A further extension of Dora's spirit.

Remember… in 1930 there was no such thing as social security or food stamps. Back then if someone did go on charity the first thing the government would do was to take the children and put them in an institution of some kind. Almost every one did every thing they could do to avoid this. When someone with children found themselves in an impoverished situation, even though they got some help from friends and family, they still had to scratch and scuffle for themselves. They had to dig in the dirt. Some could do this. Others could not. Dora did.

A Baby in the Spring

We never know what the Earth will bring.
But the next time the Flowers open their eyes
we will give them the surprise.
Because
there is going to be
A Baby in the Spring.
Don't forget to bring
the talcum and the down.
He will be a clown.
Our Baby in the Spring.
Go tell Mrs. Tree she will not be
the only one with blossoms in her hair
We will be there
with
Our Baby in the Spring.
And

they will all come to see him
little chipmunks, baby bunnies too.
Fuzzy little hiccup.
There is a smile for you.

I Am Worth Half a Hog

A study in Cracker economics

We have all heard the story about if some one were to cut up a human body and boil it down until there was nothing left except a little sediment it would contain about a dollar's worth of various elements. I can not go along with that because I know I am worth at least a half a hog.

The night I decided to make my entrance into the world my father took my mother to the hospital in the wee hours of a Sunday morning. I got there about two o'clock that afternoon in the fall of 1937. My mother and I remained in the hospital until about noon that following Friday. A four or five day stay for mother and baby at that time was customary.

The total hospital bill for the delivery room and everything was $76.40 The doctor bill was a separate $50.00. That included the monthly visits and delivery. The doctor bill was paid up by the time I got here because it was paid five or ten dollars each visit but the $76.40 hospital bill had to be paid all at once.

For the first time in his life my father was trying his hand at farming with a big ol' hog he was raising in partnership with his brother-in-law. They butchered the hog and the sale of the pork came in mighty handy when it came time to pay the hospital bill and bring my mother and me home.

My father had to drop out of college after only three years because the Great Depression had taken its toll. For five years before I was born he managed a Standard Oil gas station in Ft. Meade. He was fortunate to be in the gas station business during the depression because if any business was operating at all they needed gas. My father was doing better than most. He made $25.00 a week. He had a helper and a mechanic. They each made $15.00 a week. The station was open from 6:00 a.m. until 9:00 p.m. seven days a week.

My father thought selling the hog to get my mother and me out of the hospital was very amusing. Almost as amusing as the way he and my mother had come into enough money so they could get married two years earlier is they "hit bolita". This is a gambling game that was really against the law. My father was a tee-totaling staunch Baptist and his winning anything gambling was ironic to say the least.

When I was four years old and just before the outbreak of World War II my parents sold the gas station and their little house and we moved to Gainesville and my father went back to college. He finished a year of college and law school in about three and a half years.

The first time around the depression made it impossible for him to finish college. The second time around the war made it extremely difficult. Prices went up very high when the war broke out.

If my parents had known the war was going to start they would have not made the move and my father probably would have never become a lawyer. They made it under the wire by about two months. A move that tremendously changed our lives forever.

After my father graduated from law school we moved back home where he and my mother ran a two person law office for 35 years. Through a great deal of Cracker work ethic and tenacity theirs became one of the most successful practices in the area.

Among many other things my father became a deacon in the First Baptist church. A position that is considered to be more ecclesiastical than that of the Pope. My mother became very active in civic organizations.

Throughout it all my father remained a humble Cracker who loved to tell stories and he never let us forget the significance of "hitting bolita" and the true value of half a hog.

My Mother and Father Have an Office

The building was in the middle of the one-hundred block of Main Street directly across from the front door of the courthouse. The office was two rooms upstairs at the end of the hall beyond the dentist's office. The rooms on this floor were separated from the hallway by accordion folding French windows. The dentist had four or five rooms, my parents only two. These two rooms at the end of the hall of the old brick building had seldom been used and had not been used at all for several years. Not many people would have settled for such a remote and humble location.

It was December 1945. My father had graduated from the University of Florida law school that year and after a short stint as another lawyer's partner in Gainesville he did what he always said he wanted to do: go home and be "the best damn country lawyer there ever was."

My mother would be secretary and office manager. She had never worked in any kind of office before and was brushing up on her high school short hand and typing skills. She wanted to make a good living.

My father drove a Railway Express truck while he was finishing law school. My mother did everything she could to economize our budget. When they opened their office their ages were 30 and 34. Only four years earlier my father was manager at the Standard Oil gas station in Ft. Meade.

It is safe to say that when the two of them walked into those dingy, dirty, musty two rooms at the end of the hall they weren't quite sure where they were or it they should be there. There certainly were no signs of a successful law practice there on that day. The only thing they saw was eight walls, a floor and dirt.

My mother was born and raised on a farm in Georgia. My father was born and raised in a phosphate village. So they commenced to do what their Cracker ancestors had done since the beginning of time: lay their hands on the dirt. They got a bucket of water, rags and some kind of soap. They wiped down every bit of those two rooms, the walls, the woodwork, the windows and then, the floor. They scrubbed the floor on their hands and knees. This was partly to cleanse it and partly the Cracker ritual of making something theirs by laying on the hands of labor. Until they finished doing this they felt like the office belonged to someone else.

First, they made mud on the floor then scrubbed and wiped it up. They became one with the dirt – just like my grandparents on the farm in Georgia and my father's father at the phosphate mines. By the time they were through their hands had touched every square inch of those two rooms. Now it was theirs. Now they could begin.

One of my father's best friends gave him a desk and a bookcase. The desk had a large deep drawer that would be used as a file cabinet. They paid ten dollars for a used desk from a junk furniture store down the street for my mother. The typewriter was the old manual that had been at the gas station for years and was used when my father was in law school. A few miscellaneous chairs in case someone happened to come in they would have a place to sit down. The rent was twenty dollars a month. The only luxury in that office was a telephone. We did not have a telephone in Gainesville for four years – partly because of the war rationing and partly because we could not afford it.

So they did begin and continued to practice law for thirty-five years. Many years later they moved to a much larger office downstairs and around the corner. It was a lot fancier but it did not have the hominess and Crackerness like that first office. And, it was a treat to see my father walk down those stairs and strut across Main Street (jaywalking) into the front door of the courthouse.

He always said, "Practicing law is not work. It is fun." I guess it was compared to working on the railroad, at a feed depot, at the mines and then pounding the pavement at the gas station for nine years.

100

He loved every minute of practicing law and theirs became a very busy and successful business. Most people cannot believe this but for thirty-five years every person who came to that office got to talk to my father whether they had an appointment or not. They may have had to wait a while but they got to talk to the lawyer before they left. He took every phone call when it came in. He took calls even when he was talking to another client in his office. The only rare exception was when he was in heavy conference with several members of a family of a very complicated estate. Yes, as hard as it is to believe, he took every call when it came in and talked to every person when they came through the door. Their clients loved them.

My father was not just a lawyer. He was also a scholar. He studied law for the rest of his life. He was a lawyers' lawyer. Other lawyers and judges asked him for advice on cases. He could speak anyone's language – Black or white, country or city, educated or not. He would explain the law to the most timid, illiterate in a way they could understand it. They were beholding to him for doing this for them.

There was never, ever a time he engaged in any kind of wheeling and dealing. He was always up front, out-spoken and forthright. He was totally honest and everyone knew it.

In the meanwhile, my mother wore out manual typewriter after manual typewriter (she did not like electric ones) typing millions of words on miles of paper. She worked hard and made that good living.

They seldom charged more than the Bar Association's guidelines on minimum fees and my mother never charged anyone for notarizing signatures. Their Cracker ethics would not allow them to charge huge fees.

They became pillars of the community at church and civic organizations while serving hundreds of people with their legal work. They got a late start because of the depression and the war but both my parents succeeded in doing what they wanted to do. It is almost impossible for two people to come from where they came from, overcome such giant obstacles and wind up where they wound up. Only two

Crackers working together could have pulled this off. It is shuttering to think what everyone almost missed out on.

Most of the ritual of cleansing the office on that first day went on while I was at school. I was eight years old and trying to get a grip on the third grade in a new town. They were still working when I got there that afternoon. They were on their hands and knees scrubbing the floor when a Black woman came to the office and stood there in the doorway. She looked down at them. They looked up at her.

She had been sent by the long established lawyer on the other side of the stairwell. He had a huge office and had been there for over twenty-five years. The woman wanted to get a divorce. She went to the big lawyer first. He told her he did not have any time to spare but recommended the new lawyer across the stairwell at the end of the hall.

There was no heat. It was a cold day in December and colder on the wet floor. My father accepted her case from the muddy water in the empty office. She was grateful. He was grateful. She would pay a fee of about fifty dollars – half to begin the other half later.

We always remembered her name. It was Ruby Cooper. The first to come to the lawyer at the end of the hall. My mother and father's office.

Patchwork Quilt

I'd been rambling around
when I passed through town
and I came down with the flu.
So I laid around at mama's house
just like I used to do.
I'd been gone
it had been so long
but I sure liked where I laid –
Sleeping on my old bed
with the patchwork quilt
my mama made.
Patchwork quilt you're a beauty
run my fingers over the years.
Daddy's vest
Sister's dress
Mama's skirt

and Brother's shirt.
I had forgotten the kitchen curtains
once were blue.
And I never could figure
why Mama would sit and sew by finger
all those bits and pieces of
brightly colored cloth.
I said I'd give her the money
she said no this way honey
you'll have something of me after
I am gone.
Patchwork quilt you're a beauty
run my finger right on down.
I see Grandpa's tie
a Christmas doll
and my old wedding gown.
I've been running around
I don't have any kids
because I never would settle down.
I don't have what it takes
so I'll never make
a patchwork quilt.

Now it really does figure
why Mama would sit and sew by finger
all those bits and pieces
of brightly colored cloth.
As I lay here and rest
I see my quilt is the best
because she lined it with
the one that Grandma had made for her.
Patchwork quilt you're a beauty
run my fingers over the years.

Cracker Dog – Cracker Boy

Cracker Mama and Cracker Daddy
living in Auburndale
traveling to Frostproof
to pick up a puppy
friends had promised them
drove through Ft. Meade
across Peace River

Looking over the pups
they seemed much the same
except one so black
the sun on his coat
shined blue

He was the littlest
but when they reached

to him
he jumped back and growled
brave as a tiger
thought he was big
as a mule
Cracker Daddy said
"We have to have this one
he is a Cracker Dog
if there ever was one"
Driving back home
the puppy sniffing around
in the car
they stopped at the river
so he could
run and poo
and
run and poo

Walking by the river
in that beautiful black mud
watching the flow
saw some minnows

a speck jumped

Cypress trees standing guard
long beards of moss
hanging down
prettier than a picture
a perfect place to be

Along came floating
something the size of
a foot tub

What is it?
the Daddy cut a long pole
fished is to the bank.

It is a baby child
in a basket
woven out of
palmetto leaves

God must have put him there

When the Mama reached
to him
he let out a howl
and a kick
Cracker Mama said
"Looks like a Cracker Baby
to me
we are going to have him home with us"
named him Carl

The Cracker Mama and the Cracker Daddy
raised the Cracker Boy
named Carl
with the Cracker Dog
named Blue
together
in Auburndale.

Georgia Rain

It sure feels good
walking in Georgia rain
It soothes me with its
soppin' coolness.
It is good company –
like a friend who knows me.

I've walked in the other rain
but it did not feel the same.
Perhaps if the sun were burning me
there would be something spurning me.
But right now it sure feels mighty good
walking in Georgia rain.

Drove all the way from South Florida
to see what you meant

when you said you were
flattered by my call.
It appears you did not mean
anything at all –
like a stranger who doesn't know me.

But the rain feels mighty good.
Someday when you are not here
I will come back again –
and just
walk in Georgia rain.

A Further Attempt to Try to Sorta Explain a Few Things...Maybe

Long ago the New England states were settled mostly by people from England. That is why we call these states in the northeast "New England". That is simple enough.

These people brought their British culture with them – their attitudes, beliefs, mannerisms, habits, social activities, morals, mores and whatever else defines a strong culture. They did a good job of remaining very British.

Back in Europe, the Irish and the British were and are still at odds. The Scots are also ancient enemies of England. There has been so much bitterness between England and these countries for such a long time no one really remembers why they dislike each other so much. It doesn't really matter exactly why. When one country believes another country has held it in oppression the hatred lives on. Forever. Attitudes continue.

When the Irish came flooding into America the ones who settled in New York or there abouts were brutally discriminated against. In order to survive, some of the Irish would blend in with the British. Those who refused to blend in got absolutely no where except crushed in the gutter because they were considered to be the bilge of society just as when they were in Ireland.

These cultures were and still are very different. The British were stiff and strict, worked all the time, tried to see how much money they could make and really didn't seem to know how to enjoy life and have a good time with their friends. People of a few words.

On the other had, the Irish had a passion for their friends, singing and dancing, a magnificent gift of gab and story telling. Irish people celebrate everything, even the smallest of things. (Dr. Sigmond Freud once said, "My theories do not work on the Irish. They invert everything.") Although they worked enough, the Irish loved to entertain and to be entertained. The Southern Scots-Irish always made sure they had plenty of casual time to spend with their friends that included lots of food, music and booze.

The Irish made a point of seeing how much fun they could have. The British made a point of seeing how much fun they could not have and did not want anyone else to have any fun either. Heaven help the Irish who settled in New York and refused to become anglicized.

The Irish who flooded to America in the 1800's and settled in the Southern states kept their Irish culture. Their good old Celtic ways prevailed. This included the people from Scotland who were fortunate enough to nix New York. The South could have been called New Ireland or New Scotland. When someone from England settled in the Carolinas, Georgia, Alabama, or Florida they in reverse would tend to blend in with the Celtic culture.

From the onset the British in the North looked

upon the Scots-Irish in the South as ignorant, sloven, sloth, unkempt, inept, rowdy, immoral, lazy, drunken and worthless. The Scots-Irish in the South replied only with: "So what?!". The attitude of the North was that the South needed to be straightened out. This was not well taken by the South. Attitudes continued.

The Scots-Irish of the South lived to preserve their culture and to make sure it did not become anglicized and that included enjoying life and each other. They were not motivated by seeing how much money they could make. They lived for pleasures. The Southern people worked but reserved plenty of time for leisure. Sunday in New England was church most the day then quiet reverence at home, very quiet. Church in the South was over by noon and the rest of the day was as rowdy and festive as Saturday night.

A general consensus is that everything about the North and the South was opposite. The English in the North stressed a lot of formal education. The Scots-Irish in the South shunned formal education but stressed oral history, music and poetry, and were great story tellers. They did not want the English to come down here and run schools and anglicize their children. Text books were written from a very Northern viewpoint. When a Southern family would acquiesce and send their children to schools in the North, the first thing the Northern teachers would do was try to brain wash the Southern students. Parents would snatch their children from the schools. The North was trying to change the South and has continued to try to do so. It is very note worthy that no one has ever tried to change the North.

The Northern people continued to condemn the Southerns as being ignorant and immoral. They may not have had as much formal education but they were not low in intelligence. Northerners equated enjoying life with being dumb. As for the light footedness among married or unmarried adults, the lack of morals then was about the same as it is now. North and South.

The British have traditionally been thought as stoic. The Scots-Irish are well remembered to be prone to violence. "The Fighting Irish" means exactly that. Opposites lead to conflicts. Conflicts lead to enemies. The biggest conflict between North and the Old South had to do with government. Representatives from the Southern states were squelched in congress. They were not given as much voice as the Northern Representatives, or any voice at all.

Southern states' tremendous volume of agriculture products were taxed at a lop-sided rate. The South wanted to do business directly with Europe. The North or Federal government was determined not to let them do this. It got to a point where the North and the South were like two different countries that did not get along at all. They really did not like each other one whit. The South saw the North as being uppity and prejudiced against them. That is all it took to raise the ire of the Scots-Irish. They Rebelled for Southern Independence. Some people call this the Civil War. Slavery was an issue but it was far from the only issue. Many people are convinced the Civil War would have taken place even if there had been no such thing as slavery. Common sense should tell anyone that 600,000 white men would never go out into the prairie and murder each other solely over slavery one way or the other. Not then. Not now.

The cause of the Civil War was resentment. The North historically insulted the South for too long and for too many times. There is no one more proud than the Scots-Irish and no one quicker to defend that pride. The North saw themselves as the government and saw the South as the governed.

The Civil War was a cultural war that can be considered as an extension of the historical conflict between Ireland and England. The same soldiers who died wearing the Confederate uniform were the same soldiers who would have "died for Ireland". The Civil War was a grudge match that should have never happened. The Federal government probably could have prevented the war with diplomacy but it failed to do so. The Federal government should have banned slavery long before the war but again it failed to do so. The plight of Black people probably would have been a lot less harsh had they been freed without a war.

Before it was over the Civil War turned into an insane blood bath that was beyond everything: government, slavery, religion, politics, geography and opinion. There is yet to be a complete healing. Some white Southerners blame the Federal government and Black people for their plight. Black people blame white people for their plight. Some Yankees still believe white and Black Southerners are dumb and pitiful and need to be improved upon.

So the cultural war continues, at least in part. While most Yankees who move down here are kind and useful, there are many who tell us we are dumb, do things wrong, they do everything right "back home" and they are going to show us how everything should be done. Some are still coming down here and taking a whack at us.

It would be so nice if they would not do this.

NOTE: the Scots-Irish people in this essay are the people we call Crackers.

HISTORICAL REFERENCE: <u>Cracker Culture: Celtic Ways in the Old South,</u> Grady McWhiney, University of Alabama Press.

(A most highly recommended book)

Mama Brought the Last Crop In

Mama and Papa married
in the fall of ought three
Grandpa gave them sixty acres
free and clear

Started out on a farm
all their own
built a big fine house
a bigger fine barn

Three families of helpers lived
in little houses
near by
They had been freed
in eighteen sixty-five

but
they stayed right on
doing the hardest, harshest work

Mama and Papa brought the first crop in
together
they brought the first crop in
side by side
It wasn't too hard
with
the Freedmen's help
they brought the first crop in
together

But

Twenty-three years and nine children later
everything was gone

Papa stubbed his toe
on a bottle of something
and

that was the end of the farm

Papa drank it up
ran it down
into the ground

In nineteen-twenty-six
the bank got it all
the crop, sixty acres, the house
and
the barn
the fine farm was all gone

Lord only knows what happened
to the Freedmen
they would have stayed right on
didn't have anywhere else to go

Mama and Papa spent
their last two years
in Georgia
share cropping

on another mans land
down the road.

There were no Freedmen
to help
Papa's body all racked
and brittle
didn't make it through
the third year

Then

Mama brought the last crop in
all by herself
Mama brought the last crop in
all alone

Widow woman with five children
at home
the oldest
too selfish to help
the youngest

too young for anything
the other two
she sent to school
then
Mama brought the last crop in
all by herself

Poor woman
digging in rich dirt
curing tobacco
in a hell hot barn
picking cotton
with the best of them
grubbing peanuts
with the rest of them

Mama brought the last crop in
all by herself
got the bills paid
left the father of her children
in the forgiving Georgia ground

Took her children
down to Florida
where
her eldest had a paycheck
with
phosphate dust on it
Never to see Georgia again
travelin' in the rain

After

Mama brought the last crop in
all by herself
after
Mama brought the last crop in
all alone
-Amen

REFERENCES

Cracker Culture: Celtic Ways in the Old South, Grady McWhiney, University of Alabama Press, 1988.

Mules and Men, Zora Neal Hurston, New York, Harper Perenial, 1990, page 28.

Websters Third New International Dictionary, 1966.

The Sit-Com, "As Time Goes By", PBS, Channel 3, WEDU, Tampa, Florida, 1999.

"The Life and Death of King John", William Shakespeare, 1596, Act II, Scene 1.

Compact Edition of the Oxford English Dictionary, Oxford University Press, 1971.

The Ledger, Cinnamon Bair, March 21, 2000.

About the Author

Charlotte Crawford is a native of Polk County, Florida and is an eleventh generation Cracker.

Grew up in a small town where people did not lock their doors and the high school produced many state-wide and national notables, over-achieving doctors and incredibly talented musicians. Her life around phosphate villages is invaluable to her ability to write about Cracker lore.

She has led the typical quirky and varied life of a future writer... engineering drawing, accountant, real estate broker and a long stint in community theatre. Has written and performed songs and comedy. Considers herself to be a story teller and author. A graduate of Florida Atlantic University. Changed her major so many times she has a minor's worth is just about everything.

Author of the Play, "By Choice or Otherwise", the book, "If You Are a Cracker", books in progress: "The Ballad of Rocky Stone" and "Sterling".